T0368100

JESUS SENT YOUR HEALING— NOW RECEIVE IT

Bruce Grant

WESTBOW
P R E S S®
A DIVISION OF THOMAS NELSON
& ZONDERVAN

WestBow Press books may be ordered through booksellers or by contacting:

WestBow Press
A Division of Thomas Nelson & Zondervan
1663 Liberty Drive
Bloomington, IN 47403
www.westbowpress.com
844-714-3454

ISBN: 979-8-3850-3420-8 (sc)
ISBN: 979-8-3850-3421-5 (hc)
ISBN: 979-8-3850-3419-2 (e)

Library of Congress Control Number: 2024920041

Print information available on the last page.

WestBow Press rev. date: 09/28/2024

DISCLAIMER

I am not a doctor. This book is not meant to treat or diagnose any illnesses. It is for educational purposes only, and I am not responsible for any individual's healing.

I cannot guarantee any diseases will be healed or prevented. However, according to 1 Thessalonians 5:23, I believe that we are beings with spirits and souls, living in bodies.

Additionally, I believe that most problems are rooted in the spirit and that Jesus has died for our healing (Isaiah 53:5 and 1 Peter 2:24). I believe that God is the same God all the time, today tomorrow, and forever.

CONTENTS

INTRODUCTION

The original title of this book was *Your Healing Is on the Way*. But one night I was awakened suddenly in the middle of the night, and the thought that entered my mind was, *How can something be on the way if it is already here?* So I jumped out of the bed and went downstairs to my computer to change the title of this book to *Jesus Sent Your Healing—Now Receive It*. I have been through just about every sickness you can imagine, and the Lord has delivered me through every one of them. I have stood in long prayer lines throughout America praying for a healing. No one likes to be sick, and I felt like I was suffering from some sort of sickness all the time until, one day, I went to visit a Kenneth Hagin crusade in California. I can still remember it as though it were yesterday, when in fact it was in 1984. This was where I learned how to start praying to God for myself, and I started reading the word of God to see what God had to say about healing. I found every scripture in the Bible on healing, at least thirty-five of them, and I began to meditate upon them day and night until I memorized them.

I would quote those scriptures at least three times a day to myself. It was just like taking medicine for my healing to manifest. I continued doing this for at least a year. Then I stopped after I started getting well. About fifteen years later, all of my symptoms started showing up once again, so I went back to the scriptures and had to rememorize them because I had forgotten them. Whatever you don't use, you lose. Once again, I began to quote and meditate upon these healing scriptures until I was well. And then once again, I began to let up until, one morning, the Holy Spirit spoke to me, saying I should restart quoting those healing scriptures daily. So I did. And believe me when I say that, every time I receive a doctor's report, I just shout for joy. I thank God for His goodness because there have been times in my life when every doctor's report looked bad, and I know without doubt that it is because of my being obedient and continuing to meditate upon God's word every day that that is no longer the case. What do you have to lose? Nothing but your sickness.

Chapter 1

PRAYER OF REPENTANCE

First of all, you have to realize that, no matter what, God loves you! The Bible says, "God so loves the world that he gave his only begotten son, and that whosoever believes in him shall not perish but have eternal life" (John 3:16 KJV).

All of us have done or thought things that are wrong. This is called sin, and our sins have separated us from God. God sent His only Son, Jesus Christ, to die for our sins. Jesus lived a sinless life and then died on the cross to pay the penalty for our sins. God demonstrates His own love for us in that, while we were yet sinners, Christ died for us. Jesus rose from the dead, and now He lives in heaven with God, His Father. He offers us the gift of eternal life, of living forever with Him in heaven, if we accept him as our Lord and Savior. Jesus said, "I am the way and the truth and the life" (John 14:6 KJV).

"No one comes to the father except by me" (John 14:6). God reaches out in love to you and wants you to be His child. As many as received Him, to them He gave the right to become children of God, even to those who believe in His name. You can choose to ask Jesus Christ to forgive your sins and come into your life as your Lord and Savior.

If you want to accept Jesus Christ as your Savior and turn from your sins, you can ask Him to be your Savior and Lord by praying a prayer like this: "Lord Jesus, I believe you are the son of God. Thank you for dying on the cross for my sins. Please forgive my sins and give me the gift of eternal life. I ask you into my life and heart to be my Lord and Savior. I want to serve you always."

Chapter 2

YOU NEED TO FORGIVE
AND LET GO

"**F**or if you forgive men when they sin against you, your heavenly Father will also forgive you. But if you do not forgive men their sins, your Father will not forgive your sins" (Matthew 6:14–15). You can pray a prayer of forgiveness for others, like this: "Father, I choose to forgive them for what they did to me. It is sin, and I ask you, Father, to take this sin from them and put it on the cross. On the day of judgment when I stand before your throne, I will hold no accusation against them. Father, I ask you to bless them in Jesus's name." I know that this may seem very hard to do now. But think about it: is this person's action that you're holding onto worth your not receiving your healing?

Pray and ask the Holy Spirit to help you. He wants to remove all of your past hurts and restore you completely. But in order to do this, you must release them and let it go. The enemy would like to keep you bitter, angry, in tears, and essentially paralyzed.

Chapter 3

THE REASON YOU'RE SICK

To find out why people get sick, we would have to go back to the Garden of Eden. "In the day" can sometimes simply mean "when" in Hebrew (Genesis 2:4; Joshua 14:11; Jeremiah 7:22). But in this case "in the day" is probably stressing immediacy because the eating of the apple—which caused the effect—occurred during the day. The day that they ate the fruit, they were destined to die.

People speculate about whether this means one of two things: that they were made "very good" but were actually already mortal and had to eat the fruit of the tree of life to stay alive or that there was an actual change from being "very good" to the current state of humankind, which is not "very good." Either way, it doesn't change the point of the narrative.

Adam and Eve were created in a state that is outside our common experience now. Now we only know two states—either sinful and mortal (like us) or sinless, then raised and glorified, and now immortal (like Christ). Adam and Eve were created in a gray area, a situation where they had not yet chosen between sin and obedience.

There is only one answer, and that is sin. When Jesus spoke to the crippled man who was healed, He confirmed that sin causes sickness.

Afterward, Jesus found him in the temple and said to him, "See, you are well again. Stop sinning or something worse may happen to you" (John 5:14). Paul confirmed this also. When he was talking to Christians about the way they took communion, he said, "That is why many among you are weak and sick, and a number of you have fallen asleep" (1 Corinthians 11:30).

> Jesus called his twelve disciples to Him, sent them out, and gave them authority to drive out impure spirits and to heal every disease and sickness. (Luke 9:1)

> "Jesus Christ is the same yesterday and today and forever." (Hebrews 13:8 NKJV)

> "Most assuredly, I say to you, he who believes in Me, the works that I do he will do also; and greater works than these he will do, because I go to My Father." (John 14:12 NKJV)

> "And these signs will follow those who believe: In My name they will cast out demons; they will speak with new tongues; they will take up serpents; and if they drink anything deadly, it will by no means hurt them; they will lay hands on the sick, and they will recover." (Mark 16:17–18 NKJV) (Instantaneous healings do occur, but not every time. Mark 16:18 does not mention how long recovery will take—only that they will recover.)

> "And he took him by the right hand and lifted him up, and immediately his feet and ankle bones received strength." (Acts 3:7 NKJV)

> "For unclean spirits, crying with a loud voice, came out of many who were possessed; and many who were paralyzed and lame were healed." (Acts 8:7 NKJV)

"And Ananias went his way and entered the house; and laying his hands on him he said, 'Brother Saul, the Lord Jesus, who appeared to you on the road as you came, has sent me that you may receive your sight and be filled with the Holy Spirit.'" (Acts 9:17 NKJV)

"Immediately there fell from his eyes something like scales, and he received his sight at once; and he arose and was baptized." (Acts 9:18 NKJV)

"And it happened that the father of Publius lay sick of a fever and dysentery. Paul went in to him and prayed, and he laid his hands on him and healed him." (Acts 28:8 NKJV)

"So when this was done, the rest of those on the island who had diseases also came and were healed." (Acts 28:9 NKJV)

I believe that good health and long life are basic gifts of God to His people, especially His followers. Things go wrong, of course—sin and environmental factors have their part in this life—but God's beautiful creation (our body) was made to heal itself and to listen closely to the voice of God.

It not only listens closely to God's still, small voice, but it hears our own voices loud and clear! We speak a constant stream of negative, hateful, hurtful things every day and voice loudly our strong beliefs in death and disease.

If you were to watch carefully what you say for a week and make a note of every nod you give to someone else's opinion on death and sickness, you'd see that your mind and body are inundated with instructions to destruct! So it's very important to stay away from negative people, no matter how well meaning they are. Don't listen to television about health issues, not even commercials. They reinforce belief in death, even when they are about places to go for healing.

Unfortunately, we work so hard to sabotage ourselves. We get hurt feelings, we make mistakes, we see others succeeding while we appear to fail, and we heap on ourselves *more* self-destructive, low self-esteem verbiage. We believe we're not as good as someone else, we don't deserve this or that, we can't have this or that—you get the picture! And every negative word or thought strengthens our bodies' intentions to self-destruct.

It is not God's will for us to be sick or have accidents. God created us perfect, in His image, to be indestructible. Although we're given just 120 years for our lives (see Genesis), nowhere does scripture say that humans must be sick during life or get sick to die.

There are no victims. God gave dominion of this planet and our bodies to us. Whom do *you* blame when something goes wrong? Hopefully you've matured to the stage where you accept each moment as it is and ask what can be learned from this experience and how you can use it to help your fellow humans.

All illnesses and accidents are purposeful. This means that they fulfill a purpose. You may not be consciously aware of how your illness is serving you, but you alone are the one who will decide when you're tired of illness and ready to move into health.

Illness is often the result of an error in a thought process. All emotion draws in like kind to you. Whatever patterns of emotion you have result in life or death. Stress, anxiety, guilt or shame, self-hate, and self-punishment naturally are negative and draw death. If you correct that error in your thoughts, be assured that your body will correct its condition.

Illness is reversible. Just as the body changed *into* illness, it can change back to *health*. Your cells are aware and in communication with your soul at every moment. They are like mini brains all working in unison with your subconscious wishes and most heartfelt words.

Denial does not cure illness. You must take authority over your body and life. Most likely you have been sick because you've been denying something your heart has been trying to tell you for too long. It's easy to let life float by you without having to push an oar or steer your boat, but if that's all you're doing, don't be surprised if you're headed for the edge of a giant waterfall.

Illness is often a signal from your spirit that something is not working in your life. Learn to listen to your body and heart; you are the best lie detector system on the planet! Use this gauge: Ask yourself if a certain decision will result in comfort and happiness for you and those around you. If you *feel* a sense of comfort or happiness as you think about it, proceed. You can also use this to ask your body what you need. Always move toward your inner joy and away from pain or stress.

Think about each one of these. Even if you can't imagine that you *aren't* a victim of your illness or disease, realize that you *had* to participate in your illness or at least take your hands off the wheel, so to speak, to allow it to get started. You might try to ask your inner wisdom to tell you what purpose might this illness accomplish. What does it do for you or prevent you from having to do?

If the illness weren't there, where would you be? Or what emotions and events in your past brought this about? If there *is* something wrong in your life that your body would want to bring your attention to, what would it be and what should you be doing to set things right? I believe that many illnesses and conditions are brought on by a spiritual attack, but some are clearly self-induced. In the case of weight problems, people have been doing this to themselves for years. Death by overeating! Don't laugh—it exists.

Chapter 4

WHAT TO DO WHEN YOU RECEIVE BAD NEWS

People react to grave health news differently. Some get angry; others shrivel up in self-pity. Some people lose their faith in God; others find it. Some families fall apart; others draw closer together. What all have in common is anguish and confusion about what to do next.

In my own case, every time I received a serious diagnosis, I was stunned and devastated. Yet I knew I had to learn about my condition and the treatment decisions I had to make.

When your life is knocked off-kilter, your best hope of returning to health depends on your resilience and resourcefulness to get what you need. Be aware that you won't always feel the way you feel at first. "In the beginning, there's so much confusion and fear that it's hard to believe you'll ever get a handle on it. "But you will, and when you learn about your condition and treatment plan, your mental state will improve and you'll likely find strength you didn't know you had."

Take your time. Unless you're in a hospital emergency room and have to make an immediate decision, don't rush into treatment until you have gotten a second opinion and more information. "Of course, your doctor will advise you, but in the end it will be up to you to decide between one treatment plan or another, between one specialist or another, between a hospital that's close to home or one that gives better treatment but is far away."

Choose whom you tell. It's a good time to move slowly and protect your privacy. Share your situation with people who will be helpful and who will offer support and comfort. That said, the mental and emotional challenges brought on by serious illness are considerable for the person with the disease and for his or her family, and at times family members may not be up to the task of providing all the support that's needed. In these situations, you may find it helpful to talk with a trusted therapist or spiritual adviser who can act as a sounding board as well as a guide through the difficult days ahead.

In the midst of all this turmoil, it's important to know that you are more than your disease. Although serious illness can shatter your sense of control, it doesn't mean the strength and knowledge you have attained in your life are irrelevant to the challenge you now face. You're the same person you were before your diagnosis, and your history, experiences, and wisdom remain. Your aim at this moment is to make it through with all the grace you can muster, all the support you can find, and all the dignity you deserve.

> Do not fear, for I am with you; Do not anxiously look about you, for I am your God. I will strengthen you, surely I will help you, surely I will uphold you with My righteous right hand. (Isaiah 41:10 KJV)

> The LORD is my light and my salvation; Whom shall I fear? The LORD is the defense of my life; Whom shall I dread? (Psalm 27:1 KJV)

> And my God shall supply all your needs according to His riches in glory in Christ Jesus. (Philippians 4:19 KJV)

Be anxious for nothing, but in everything by prayer and supplication with "thanksgiving" let your requests be made known to God. And the peace of God, which surpasses all comprehension, shall guard your hearts and your minds in Christ Jesus. Finally, brethren, whatever is true, whatever is honorable, whatever is right, whatever is pure, whatever is lovely, whatever is of good report, if there is any excellence and if anything worthy of praise, let your mind dwell on these things. (Philippians 4:6–8 KJV)

"For I know the plans that I have for you," declares the LORD, "plans for welfare and not for calamity to give you a future and a hope. Then you will call upon Me and come and pray to Me, and I will listen to you. And you will seek Me and find Me, when you search for Me with all your heart." (Jeremiah 29:11–13 KJV)

Blessed is the man who trusts in the LORD And whose trust is the LORD. For he will be like a tree planted by the water, That extends its roots by a stream And will not fear when the heat comes; But its leaves will be green, And it will not be anxious in a year of drought Nor cease to yield fruit. (Jeremiah 17:7–8 KJV)

The LORD also will be a stronghold for the oppressed, A stronghold in times of trouble, And those who know Thy name will put their trust in Thee; For Thou, O LORD, hast not forsaken those who seek Thee. (Psalm 9:9–10 KJV)

Come to Me, all who are weary and heavy-laden, and I will give you rest. Take My yoke upon you, and learn from

Me, for I am gentle and humble in heart; and you shall find rest for your souls. For My yoke is easy, and My load is light. (Matthew 11:28–30 KJV)

Therefore we do not lose heart, but though our outer man is decaying, yet our inner man is being renewed day by day. For momentary, light affliction is producing for us an eternal weight of glory far beyond all comparison, while we look not at the things which are seen, but at the things which are not seen; for the things which are seen are temporal, but the things which are not seen are eternal. (2 Corinthians 4:16–18 KJV)

For I consider that the sufferings of this present time are not worthy to be compared with the glory that is to be revealed to us. (Romans 8:18 KJV)

The LORD is my rock and my fortress and my deliverer, my God, my rock, in whom I take refuge, my shield, and the horn of my salvation, my stronghold. (Psalm 18:2 KJV)

The LORD is near to the brokenhearted and saves the crushed in spirit. (Psalm 34:18 KJV)

For because he himself has suffered when tempted, he is able to help those who are being tempted. (Hebrews 2:18 KJV)

As it is, I rejoice, not because you were grieved, but because you were grieved into repenting. For you felt a godly grief, so that you suffered no loss through us. For godly grief produces a repentance that leads to salvation without regret, whereas worldly grief produces death. (2 Corinthians 7:9–10 KJV)

And he said, "Naked I came from my mother's womb, and naked shall I return. The LORD gave, and the LORD has taken away; blessed be the name of the LORD." (Job 1:21 KJV)

They will see his face, and his name will be on their foreheads. And night will be no more. They will need no light of lamp or sun, for the Lord God will be their light, and they will reign forever and ever. (Revelation 22:4–5 KJV)

This would be my comfort; I would even exult in pain unsparing, for I have not denied the words of the Holy One. (Job 6:10 KJV)

No temptation has overtaken you that is not common to man. God is faithful, and he will not let you be tempted beyond your ability, but with the temptation he will also provide the way of escape, that you may be able to endure it. (1 Corinthians 10:13 KJV)

Resist him, stand firm in your faith, knowing that the same kinds of suffering are being experienced by your brotherhood throughout the world. And after you have suffered a little while, the God of all grace, who has called you to his eternal glory in Christ, will himself restore, confirm, strengthen, and establish you. (1 Peter 5:9–10 KJV)

Have you not known? Have you not heard? The LORD is the everlasting God, the Creator of the ends of the earth. He does not faint or grow weary; his understanding is unsearchable. He gives power to the faint, and to him who has no might he increases strength. Even youths shall faint and be weary, and young men shall fall exhausted; but they who wait for the LORD shall renew their strength; they shall mount up with wings like eagles; they shall run and not be weary; they shall walk and not faint. (Isaiah 40:28–31 KJV)

Chapter 5

YOU HAVE TO BE DETERMINED
TO BE HEALED

Now, we are at the threshold of a turn of events in the gospel of John, after the introduction of the word and the miracles that proved Christ's claims, and we see the events that led to our Lord's Passion. We see an encounter with a sick man that rattles the comfort zone of the religious leaders to the point that they seek the destruction of Christ.

For thirty-eight years, a man sat by a pool that supposedly had healing properties. He sat and was determined to be healed, but somehow he was not able to get into the water. He was a man with all kinds of excuses and reasons as to why he could not get in and get on with his life.

He faced a barrier to growing further, a choice concerning doing more with his life and his relationship to God, and he chose to sit and wait; the result was nothing but despair and excuses. So what did our Lord say to this man, one who had lost all hope, that caused such a fervent response from the religious leaders?

Do you want to be healed? This is a seemingly strange question, for who would not want to be healed or restored to a better place in life? This healing brings our Lord toe to toe with the religious leaders of His day.

They ignore their own law while they lift up their presumptions and rules as if they were gods and, in so doing, repress the truth. The uproar ultimately leads to our Lord's persecution and crucifixion. The events of the healing take place at a pool to which people flocked for healing. You may have seen news stories about an image of the Virgin Mary attracting swarms of devotees claiming healing and miracles or a TV preacher who waves his hands and utters phrases as people fall backward, claiming to be healed.

These places for healing were very popular. Perhaps the mineral salts and the hot temperature provided the body with the nutrients needed to promote healing; perhaps it was just psychosomatic; but, culturally, it was a place to go to be made well. During our Lord's time on earth, before modern hospitals and medicine, these places for healing overflowed with people who were desperately seeking relief from their ills.

They were called healing shrines and were common in the ancient world. Jesus stopped by at a time when the pool was even more crowded than usual, as the people were hoping for an extra miracle of healing because of the upcoming feast day, possibly the Feast of the Tabernacles (Exodus 23:16; 34:22; Leviticus 23:34–43; Numbers 29:12–40; Deuteronomy 16:13–16).

It is interesting to point out that this pool of Bethesda was considered a myth by liberal attackers of the Bible until it was discovered and excavated around 1967. The pool is located in the north part of the Temple Mount, near what was called Sheep Gate––just as the Bible described. There you might be, sitting in a mineral bath and wondering what that smell was, and then you would realize it was because of all the sheep going in and out right beside you!

Undoubtedly, healings did occur there. Just as today, healings take place in these special areas where people go believing they can be healed. They are very powerful, motivational, and psychological events.

When people believe they are going to be healed, go to a place where healings supposedly occur, and do the expected thing, many of them are healed. Perhaps it is a miracle, as I believe; perhaps some fake it for attention;

while others are only temporarily healed as their willpower overtakes their symptoms for a while. Thus, the pool at Bethesda had established a reputation as a place where people could be healed. The man who sat outside labored for thirty-eight years to get in the water first so he could be healed—a seeming example of sheer determination and perseverance. I used to think that this man lay at the pool at Bethesda for thirty-eight years, but the Bible does not say that; it says he had been ill for thirty-eight years.

We do not know why, but he probably had some kind of wasting disease—perhaps cancer, tuberculosis, or multiple sclerosis. Some ailment immobilized him and prevented him from walking, or at least walking well enough to get where he wanted or needed to be. In any event, his disease made him unable to walk for thirty-eight years, almost as long as his ancestors had wandered in the desert.

So there was a great crowd of people—paralyzed, blind, lame, sick—all waiting for the water to be stirred. Out of that crowd Jesus picked one man. He did not empty the five porches, healing everybody. He did not invite them all to come down so that He might lay hands on them; He went to only one man. Perhaps because he was the neediest and the most helpless, Jesus was drawn to him; after thirty-eight years of illness, he would seem to fit the bill.

Perhaps we can see ourselves in a similar situation; perhaps you are in a similar situation and are physically ill or stuck in your journey of life. You may not be literally in a healing shrine, but you feel incapacitated in your spiritual walk or stagnant in your life to the point that you feel helpless, weak, crippled, and lame.

Whether you are literally lying at a healing shrine or seeking a change from the situation you are in now, you need help. We all find ourselves paralyzed at times, unable to do the thing we want or should do or what we are called to do.

Maybe we have come to a barrier in our spiritual growth that has stopped us dead in our tracks. We can see where we need to go, but we have no idea how to get there. We have hit a roadblock where the Lord has called us to go in our spiritual journey and growth. We have come face to face with a barrier that lames us; thus, spiritually, we cannot walk very well.

John goes on to say what Jesus did. When Jesus saw him lying there and learned that he had been in this condition for a long time, He asked him, "Do you want to get well?" (John 5:6 NIV).

Maybe you are thinking, *What a strange question that was to ask of a man who had been sick for thirty-eight years—"Do you want to get well?" How could someone not want to be healed?* After all, he showed his persistence. But Jesus never asked a silly or irrelevant question. Obviously, this question was important for this man to answer; maybe it is for us, too!

The simple question is, Do we want to grow deeper in the precepts of the word and character of Christ? In other words, do we want to go through the barrier that stops us dead in our tracks? Jesus asks that question just as if we were in a twelve-step program where we had to admit our need and our higher power before we can get anywhere out of our drunken state!

Consider these stories from the Bible:

A large crowd followed and pressed around Him. And a woman was there who had been subject to bleeding for twelve years. She had suffered a great deal under the care of many doctors and had spent all she had, yet instead of getting better she grew worse. When she heard about Jesus, she came up behind Him in the crowd and touched his cloak, because she thought, "If I just touch His clothes, I will be healed." Immediately her bleeding stopped and she felt in her body that she was freed from her suffering. At once Jesus realized that power had gone out from Him. He turned around in the crowd and asked, "Who touched my clothes?" "You see the people crowding against you," His disciples answered, "and yet you can ask, 'Who touched Me?'" But Jesus kept looking around to see who had done it. Then the woman, knowing what had happened to her, came and knelt at His feet, and trembling with fear, told Him the whole truth. He said to her, "Daughter, your faith has healed you. Go in peace and be freed from your suffering." (Mark 5:25–34 KJV)

Similarly, the following story demonstrates healing by faith:

And again He entered Capernaum after *some* days, and it was heard that He was in the house. Immediately many gathered together, so that there was no longer room to receive *them*, not even near the door. And He preached the word to them. Then they came to Him, bringing a paralytic who was carried by four *men*. And when they could not come near Him because of the crowd, they uncovered the roof where He was. So when they had broken through, they let down the bed on which the paralytic was lying. (1–4)

Large crowds followed Jesus wherever He went, with some bringing their sick friends and relatives to be healed. On this day as He was leaving Jerusalem, He was again accompanied by a crowd of people.

As he drew near to Jericho they saw a blind beggar sitting by the roadside. His name was Bartimaeus. He began to shout, "Jesus, Son of David, have mercy on me!" (Jesus was called Son of David because he was a descendant of King David, who had ruled Israel for forty years many years before.)

The blind man's friends told him to be quiet, but he called out even louder to Jesus.

BRUCE GRANT

Jesus stopped and told his disciples to call Bartimaeus over to him. They said to him, "Cheer up! On your feet! He is calling you." He threw off his coat and came to Jesus. **Jesus asked him what he wanted, and he said, "Rabbi (meaning "teacher"), I want to see."**

Jesus said, "Go, your faith has healed you." Immediately, he was able to see, and he followed Jesus.

What a happy day in the life of this blind man who had believed in the healing power of the Son of God! The blind man in the story was persistent. He did not give up. He called out again and again. He would not stop until he could talk to Jesus. These events took place at a pool to which people flocked.

One time Jesus told the story of a widow who had not been treated fairly (Luke 18:1–8). She kept going back to the judge until he gave her what she wanted. Don't give up. He will help.

Chapter 6

HOW TO PRAY FOR
YOUR INFIRMITY

Whether your healing prayers are for yourself, for a family member or friend, focused on a group of individuals, or general requests for world peace, it is your intention that stirs healing into action. Prayer really does offer a powerful effect on our well-being. The intention of closed eyes during prayer is to quiet the mind, whereas the intention of two hands placed together during prayer is to quiet the physical body's activities. When the mind and hands are silenced, the spirit is allowed a more focused communication.

Places where people fall backward, claiming to be healed, were very popular. Perhaps we all know the different things that can happen to our bodies that can cause them to break down and, in some cases, seriously disable us. Just about any part of the human body can get hit with some type of cancer, and in some of these cases, these cancers can be terminal.

However, as Christians, we have an all-powerful God who not only has the power to fully heal us from any specific ailment that may strike us but who actually does want to heal us many times, if we properly approach Him in our prayers.

Many people quit praying after a while because they want prayer to work like a light switch: You flip the switch and the light comes on. People quickly learn that prayer isn't like that. Sometimes it "works," and sometimes it doesn't. Discouraged by cases where prayer seems to be ineffective, some people quit. As a result, they don't later experience cases where amazing things happen.

Life is complex. Prayer is more like baseball than a light switch. When Babe Ruth came to the plate, no one ever knew in advance what might happen. He often struck out, swinging and missing three times in a row. But if spectators watched long enough, they could be sure to see a home run. Nobody told Babe Ruth, "You need to quit. You have too many at bats where you swing and miss." No! It's *expected* in baseball that great players won't succeed in every attempt. But you also know that, if they keep at it, amazing things will happen.

When you pray, you won't be able to predict in advance which times you'll "swing and miss" and which times you'll hit home runs. But if you persist in times when nothing has worked (yet!), you'll see amazing things happen. You'll see people healed of cancer, back pain, and life-long conditions—by *your* prayers.

Ask God's power and love to flow through you. Pray every chance you get. Be open to opportunities (Numbers 29:12–40; Deuteronomy 16:13–16). Pray what God's word teaches, not your doubts. Tell the disease or the person's body what to do. Don't hedge. Be direct. And don't quit early.

I've heard people say "It's God's will" or "I'll just leave it up to God" when faced with a serious illness or tragedy. Don't fall into that trap. God wants us to pray to Him for help. Jesus told His disciples that they "should always pray and not give up." And then Jesus asked "Will not God bring about justice for his chosen ones, who cry out to him day and night?" (Luke 18:1 KJV).

Pray to God from your heart for healing. Don't stop. Don't give up. God wants us to ask Him for help. He loves us.

In Mark 11:22–25 (KJV), Jesus further instructs to forgive when we pray.

> I tell you the truth, if anyone says to this mountain, "Go, throw yourself into the sea," and does not doubt in his heart but believes that what he says will happen, it will be done for him. Therefore I tell you, whatever you ask for in prayer, believe that you have received it, and it will be yours. And when you stand praying, if you hold anything against anyone, forgive him, so that your Father in heaven may forgive you your sins.

Only someone facing or sharing a serious sickness, pain, or tragedy knows how hard it is to cope with the fear and uncertainty. They know how absurd it sounds when someone first tells them to "keep a positive attitude." They know how terrifying it is when the doubt comes. They know how hard it is to throw a mountain into the sea. But remember what Jesus told us in Matthew 17:19–20 (KJV): "I tell you the truth, if you have faith as small as a mustard seed, you can say to this mountain, 'Move from here to there' and it will move. Nothing will be impossible for you." "Faith as small as a mustard seed" sounds a little like hope to me, and that's a good start. God bless you on your healing journey.

Over 20 percent of the Gospel is about the healing ministry of Jesus Christ. He taught His disciples how to pray and heal. He sent them to carry on His work. Wouldn't Jesus want His followers to pray for healing today?

Many spiritual writers have defined the call of healing so narrowly that some people feel they don't qualify. But today a new awakening in faith has made us realize we are not only called into healing for ourselves but also in various degrees into healing one another.

The Bible actually gives us some directions on how to pray for healing. For example, in James 5:14–15 (KJV), we are told: "Is any one of you sick?

He should call the elders of the church to pray over him and anoint him with oil in the name of the Lord. And the prayer offered in faith will make the sick person well; the Lord will raise him up. If he has sinned, he will be forgiven." Then, in James 5:16 (KJV), we are told to "confess your sins to each other and pray for each other so that you may be healed" and then that "The prayer of a righteous man is powerful and effective."

Chapter 7

SCRIPTURES TO MEDITATE ON DAILY

The very first thing you will really have to grasp is how good and merciful God and Jesus really are. Every time God decides to heal someone, He is showing incredible mercy, love, goodness, and compassion toward that person. So the first things you will need to grasp from scripture are the specific verses that will show you how merciful, kind, and compassionate God the Father really is.

You have to realize that God the Father does have these attributes in His personality. If you do not believe that God the Father is a good, merciful, loving, kind, and compassionate God, then you may not be able to receive a divine healing from Him because you will not have enough faith and belief in His ability to even want to heal you in the first place.

So the first thing Christians must really grab a hold of if they want to press in for a divine healing from the Lord is that God the Father really does have a very loving and tender side to His personality—and that much of the time He actually does *want* to heal us and help deliver us out of any adverse situation that we may have just fallen into. And any kind of disease, illness, or sickness is definitely an adverse situation.

But You are God, ready to pardon, gracious and merciful, slow to anger, abundant in kindness … (Nehemiah 9:17 KJV)

The Lord is merciful and gracious, slow to anger, and abounding in mercy. (Psalm 103:8 KJV)

But You, O Lord, are a God full of compassion, and gracious, longsuffering and abundant in mercy and truth. (Psalm 86:15 KJV)

Return to the Lord your God, for He is gracious and merciful, slow to anger, and of great kindness …" (Joel 2:13 KJV)

The Lord is gracious and full of compassion, slow to anger and great in mercy. The Lord is good to all, and His tender mercies are over all His works. (Psalm 145:8 KJV)

The Lord is good; His mercy is everlasting. (Psalm 100:5 KJV)

For as the heavens are high above the earth, so great is His mercy toward those who fear Him.… But the mercy of the Lord is from everlasting to everlasting on those who fear Him. (Psalm 103:1 KJV)

God is your perfect, loving Father, and He has nothing but your best interests at heart. If you have been struck with any kind of illness or disease, do not be afraid to approach Him for a divine healing. You may be pleasantly surprised with what He might do for you. Sometimes when someone has been hit by an extreme sickness or disease, especially with one that may be considered terminal, our faith levels may be severely shaken—possibly to their core!

Imagine that you have been just diagnosed with terminal cancer, and the doctors have told you that you have only six more months to live. Though you know God is all-powerful, your situation looks so hopeless and bleak that you now start doubting whether or not God can really deliver you out of such a dire, extreme, and hopeless situation. You are so overwhelmed by the hopelessness of the situation that you start forgetting how powerful God really is and that He does have the full supernatural power to be able to fully heal you, no matter how grave the situation may appear to you in the natural.

These next three verses tell us that nothing—I repeat, nothing—is impossible for God to handle. Again, these verses should be burned into your memory bank so you can have them fully loaded in your mind and spirit if you are ever faced with what appear to be insurmountable odds.

> For with God nothing will be impossible. (Luke 1:37 KJV)

> But He said, "The things which are impossible with men are possible with God." (Luke 18:27 KJV)

> Now to Him who is able to do exceedingly abundantly above all that we ask or think, according to the power that works in us. (Ephesians 3:20 KJV)

Remember, God the Father has the full power and full ability to accomplish anything that He will want to do. If He has the full, divine, supernatural power to create our entire world in six days, then I do not think He will have any problems in being able to fully heal you of whatever sickness or disease may have just struck your body.

The Bible tells us that God the Father is no respecter of persons, which means He loves each person He has ever created equally and unconditionally. This tells us that, if both God and Jesus were healing people in the times of both the Old Testament and New Testament, then there is no reason we cannot approach Him for our own personal healing when we may need it in this day and age. Once you understand how many times God and Jesus healed other people back in both the Old and New

Testaments, then this will help build up your own faith and belief that just maybe God and Jesus can also do the exact same thing for you.

Again, study this next set of verses very, very carefully. These specific verses all show how God the Father can heal His own if they are walking in good stead with Him. This first verse is a major, foundational verse that needs to be fully committed to memory. It tells us that God the Father does not change—ever! In other words, God the Father is the same today as He was yesterday, and He will be the same for all of eternity. This is why God the Father is totally dependable.

If God the Father is the same today as He was yesterday, and if He was healing people back in the Old Testament days, then this means that He can and will continue to heal today. This is why divine healing is still for everyone in this day and age. The gift of healing did not stop after the first set of apostles left the scene. Here is the verse: "For I am the Lord, I do not change" (Malachi 3:6 KJV).

These next verses all show us the times that God the Father healed His own chosen people back in the Old Testament. If God the Father has not changed and if He was healing His own chosen people back in the Old Testament, then this means He can and will continue to heal His own chosen people in the New Testament, who are all saved and born-again Christians! The next verse specifically tells us that, if we belong to Jesus, then we are all part of "Abraham's seed" and are thus "heirs" to the same blessings that God the Father gave the Jewish people back in the Old Testament. And one of those blessings was divine healing whenever they would need it. These verses will show you how active God the Father really was in the area of divine healing when the Jewish people were walking in good stead with Him.

> And if you are Christ's, then you are Abraham's seed, and heirs according to the promise. (Galatians 3:29 KJV)

> If you diligently heed the voice of the Lord your God and do what is right in His sight, give ear to His commandments

and keep all His statutes, I will put none of the diseases on you which I have brought on the Egyptians. For I am the Lord who heals you. (Exodus 15:26 KJV)

And the Lord will take away from you all sickness, and will afflict you with none of the terrible diseases of Egypt which you have known, but will lay them on all those who hate you. (Deuteronomy 7:15 KJV)

So you shall serve the Lord your God, and He will bless your bread and your water. And I will take sickness away from the midst of you. No one shall suffer miscarriage or be barren in your land; I will fulfill the number of your days. (Exodus 23:25 KJV)

He sent His word and healed them, and delivered them from their destructions. (Psalm 107:20 KJV)

He also brought them out with silver and gold, and there was none feeble among His tribes. (Psalm 105:37 KJV)

Bless the Lord, O my soul, and forget not all His benefits: who forgives all your iniquities; who heals all your diseases. (Psalm 103:2 KJV)

Many are the afflictions of the righteous, but the Lord delivers him out of them all. He guards all his bones; not one of them is broken. (Psalm 34:19 KJV)

In these verses, we read several key phrases:

- "Put none of these diseases on you"
- "Take away from you all sickness"

- "Sent His word and healed them"
- "There was none feeble among His tribes"
- "Heals all your diseases"
- "Guards all his bones; not one of them is broken"
- "Restore health to you and heal you of your wounds"
- "Heals the brokenhearted and binds up their wounds"

Again, if God the Father did this for the Jewish people back in Old Testament times and we have a new and better covenant through His Son Jesus Christ in the New Testament, then we all should have access to the same blessings that the Jewish people had. And one of those blessings was having divine health and divine healing from Him when it was really needed.

Jesus Christ Does Want to Heal You

If all of the above verses are showing us that it was the will of God the Father to heal His chosen people back in the Old Testament, then the next set of verses will show us that it was also the will of Jesus Christ to heal when He was walking in the New Testament.

If God the Father was constantly healing His people back in the Old Testament when they were walking right with Him, then it should come as no surprise that His Son Jesus wanted to do the exact same thing as He was walking among us in the New Testament. And that is exactly what you will find. Jesus was constantly healing people who came to Him, especially when they came to Him with enough faith and belief that He could actually heal them.

Here are eleven key verses showing how active Jesus really was in the area of divine healing when He was walking with the full power of God for about three and a half years. Notice the first verse says the same thing about Jesus that a previous one did about God the Father—that He is the same today as He was yesterday. This means that, if Jesus had a desire to heal when He was walking on our earth two thousand years ago, then He will still have that same desire to heal anyone in this day and age!

Jesus Christ is the same yesterday, today, and forever. (Hebrews 13:8 KJV)

Then Jesus returned in the power of the Spirit to Galilee.... "The Spirit of the Lord is upon Me, because He has anointed Me to preach the gospel to the poor. He has sent Me to heal the brokenhearted, to preach deliverance to the captives and recovery of sight to the blind, to set at liberty those who are oppressed, to preach the acceptable year of the Lord." (Luke 4:14 KJV)

How God anointed Jesus of Nazareth with the Holy Spirit and with power, who went about doing good and healing all who were oppressed by the devil, for God was with Him. (Acts 10:38 KJV)

But when Jesus knew it, He withdrew from there; and great multitudes followed Him, and He healed them all. (Matthew 12:15 KJV)

And when Jesus went out He saw a great multitude; and He was moved with compassion for them, and healed their sick. (Matthew 14:14 KJV)

Now it happened on a certain day, as He was teaching, that there were Pharisees and teachers of the law sitting by, who had come out of every town of Galilee, Judea, and Jerusalem. And the power of the Lord was present to heal them. (Luke 5:17 KJV)

And when the men of that place recognized Him, they sent out into all that surrounding region, brought to Him all who were sick, and begged Him that they might only touch the hem of His garment. And as many as touched it were made perfectly well. (Matthew 14:35 KJV)

… who came to hear Him and be healed of their diseases, as well as those who were tormented with unclean spirits. And they were healed. And the whole multitude sought to touch Him, for power went out from Him and healed them all. (Luke 6:17 KJV)

But when the multitudes knew it, they followed Him; and He received them and spoke to them about the kingdom of God, and healed those who had need of healing. (Luke 9:11 KJV)

When evening had come, they brought to Him many who were demon-possessed. And He cast out the spirits with a word, and healed all who were sick. (Matthew 8:16 KJV)

Now Jesus went about all Galilee, teaching in their synagogues, preaching the gospel of the kingdom and healing all kinds of sickness and all kinds of diseases among the people. (Matthew 4:23 KJV)

Not only does God the Father want to heal you, not only does His Son Jesus Christ want to heal you, but now God wants to take it one step further. He now wants to anoint His believers with His supernatural power to be able to heal others.

Do you get the big picture on all of this? If God wants to anoint His believers with His supernatural power to heal others, then this tells us that

God is now placing the gift of healing as a major blessing within His body so we can have it available to us when we may need it.

The reason for this is that God wants to anoint and empower His people to go to work for Him in preaching the gospel to the rest of the world and doing what He wants them to do in their specific calls for Him. You cannot work for God at full force in this life if you are constantly battling one ailment after another. You have to be operating in some kind of good, physical health in order to max out in your specific calls and duties for the Lord.

Chapter 8

JESUS HAS ALREADY SENT YOUR HEALING—YOU JUST HAVE TO RECEIVE IT

Since we all live in a cursed and fallen world as a result of the curse of Adam and Eve, any one of us can get sick at any time. As a result, God has to have the gifts of healing operating within His body so as to help get us back up and running if we do get hit with any kind of sickness or disease. Sometimes God will choose to heal you through doctors and other medical professionals, but other times He will choose to heal you directly Himself or through the prayers of other anointed believers.

> And He said to them, "Go into all the world and preach the gospel to every creature. He who believes and is baptized will be saved; but he who does not believe will be condemned. And these signs will follow those who believe: in My name they will cast out demons; they will speak with new tongues; they will take up serpents; and if they drink anything deadly, it will by no means

hurt them; they will lay hands on the sick, and they will recover." (Mark 16:15 KJV)

Then He called His twelve disciples together and gave them power and authority over all demons, and to cure diseases. (Luke 9:1 KJV)

And He called the twelve to Him, and began to send them out two by two, and gave them power over unclean spirits.... And they cast out many demons, and anointed with oil many who were sick, and healed them. (Mark 6:7 KJV)

And when He had called His twelve disciples to Him, He gave them power over unclean spirits, to cast them out, and to heal all kinds of sickness and all kinds of disease." (Matthew 10:1 KJV)

But go rather to the lost sheep of the house of Israel. And as you go, preach saying, "The kingdom of heaven is at hand. Heal the sick, cleanse the lepers, raise the dead, cast out demons. Freely you have received, freely give." (Matthew 10:6 KJV)

Now God worked unusual miracles by the hands of Paul, so that even handkerchiefs or aprons were brought from his body to the sick, and the diseases left them and the evil spirits went out of them. (Acts 19:11 KJV)

And it happened that the father of Publius lay sick of a fever and dysentery. Paul went in to him and prayed, and he laid hands on him and healed him. (Acts 28:8 KJV)

And the multitudes with one accord heeded the things spoken by Philip, hearing and seeing the miracles which he did. For unclean spirits, crying with a loud voice, came out of many who were possessed; and many who were paralyzed and lame were healed. (Acts 8:6 KJV)

Therefore they stayed there a long time, speaking boldly in the Lord, who was bearing witness to the word of His grace, granting signs and wonders to be done by their hands. (Acts 14:3 KJV)

And I will give you the keys of the kingdom of heaven, and whatever you bind on earth will be bound in heaven, and whatever you loose on earth will be loosed in heaven. (Matthew 16:19 KJV)

Now there are diversities of gifts, but the same Spirit. There are differences of ministries, but the same Lord. And there are diversities of activities, but it is the same God who works all in all. But the manifestation of the Spirit is given to each one for the profit of all. (1 Corinthians 12:4–7 KJV)

For to one is given the word of wisdom through the Spirit, to another the word of knowledge through the same Spirit, to another faith by the same Spirit, to another gifts of healings by the same Spirit, to another the working of miracles, to another prophecy, to another discerning of spirits, to another different kinds of tongues, to another the interpretation of tongues. But one and the same Spirit works all these things, distributing to each one individually as He wills. (1 Corinthians 12:8–11 KJV)

The Power of Prayer

It is quite obvious that God the Father has the full, divine power to fully heal you of any disease or sickness that could strike your body. So how do you get God to release His healing power directly to you to heal either yourself or someone else you may be praying for? By direct prayer to God the Father. And sometimes that prayer has to be a *prevailing type of prayer,* which means that you keep praying to God until you get the healing to fully manifest onto the affected part of the body that will need the healing.

There are many different prayer strategies that you can use in your own personal prayers to the Lord. I will be discussing some of these different types of prayer strategies in other sections. But for the sake of this chapter, I will quote some specific verses that tell us that, sometimes, we have to pray directly to God the Father for a full healing to manifest. The first three verses specifically tell us to *pray* to God when we are sick and need healing.

> Is anyone among you suffering? Let him pray. (James 5:13 KJV)

> Is anyone among you sick? Let him call for the elders of the Church, and let them pray over him, anointing him with oil in the name of the Lord. And the prayer of faith will save the sick, and the Lord will raise him up. And if he has committed sins, he will be forgiven. (James 5:14 KJV)

> And it happened that the father of Publius lay sick of a fever and dysentery. Paul went in to him and prayed, and he laid his hands on him and healed him. (Acts 28:8 KJV)

> The effective, fervent prayer of a righteous man avails much. (James 5:16 KJV)

Let us therefore come boldly to the throne of grace, that we may obtain mercy and find grace to help in time of need. (Hebrews 4:16 KJV)

Ask, and it will be given to you; seek, and you will find; knock, and it will be opened to you. (Matthew 7:7 KJV)

Yet you do not have it because you do not ask. (James 4:2 KJV)

And there is no one who calls on Your name, who stirs himself up to take hold of You. (Isaiah 64:7 KJV)

So I sought for a man among them who would make a wall, and *stand in the gap before Me on behalf of the land,* that I should not destroy it; but I found no one. (Ezekiel 22:30 KJV, emphasis added)

He saw that there was no man, and *wondered if there was no intercessor;* therefore His own arm brought salvation for him. (Isaiah 59:16 KJV, emphasis added)

Therefore He said that He would destroy them, had not Moses His chosen one *stood before Him in the breach,* to turn away His wrath, lest He destroy them. (Psalm 106:23 KJV, emphasis needed)

Having Faith and Belief That God Can Actually Heal You

Sometimes God will move to heal someone who has a very low level of faith in Him, but at other times He will want the sick person to build up his or her faith a bit before He will move in with His healing power.

As you will see in the following verses, many times Jesus would ask the people He wanted to heal whether or not they had enough faith and belief in Him that He could actually heal them. Once they said they had sufficient faith in Jesus that He could heal them, then Jesus would move in to heal them.

Jesus would then tell the people that their faith was what got them healed! However, it was quite obvious that what healed them was the power of the Holy Spirit operating and manifesting through Jesus. Jesus's point was that what got the healing power from the Holy Spirit to manifest onto these people was their faith and belief that Jesus could actually do this for them.

This is how powerful of a thing it really is to get your faith operating at higher levels with the Lord. Once it is, then God can manifest bigger and greater miracles either to you or through you to help someone else out.

If you are looking for God's divine healing power to fully heal you or someone else, the first thing you will need to do is to get your personal faith levels built up to a little bit of a higher range. And how do you do this? The Bible tells us that faith comes by hearing the word of God, which means "reading the Bible" for yourself and believing what you are reading. If you are willing to do this, then the Holy Spirit will start to raise your faith to a higher level. And once your faith has been raised to that higher level, then God may move in to heal you or someone else you may be praying for.

You will need to read all of the verses pertaining to divine healing in the Bible. This chapter gives you many of these verses. Really meditate and chew on these verses. Let them sink and settle down into your mind and spirit. Believe what you are reading.

Once these verses have really settled into your mind and spirit and you truly believe what they are telling you, then go into major, prevailing prayer with the Lord to try and get Him to move in with His healing power. Quote these verses back to Him. Tell Him that you are standing on the full power and the full authority of these verses. Tell Him that you have full faith and belief in what these verses tell you.

Tell Him that you are going to take hold of Him and that you will not let Him go until He heals you or someone else you may be praying for. Again, a much more in-depth chapter will follow on the power of prevailing prayer with the Lord, especially when you are looking for a major miracle from Him.

But study these next verses very carefully. You are being given a major prayer secret from the Lord on how to get Him to move in with His healing power, and that secret is that your faith must operate at a higher level so you will believe that God can really heal you.

> Now faith is the substance of things hoped for, the evidence of things not seen. (Hebrews 11:1 KJV)

> So then faith comes by hearing, and hearing by the word of God. (Romans 10:17 KJV)

> But without faith it is impossible to please Him, for he who comes to God must believe that He is, and that He is a rewarder of those who diligently seek Him. (Hebrews 11:6 KJV)

> For whatever is born of God overcomes the world. And this is the victory that has overcome the world—our faith. (1 John 5:4 KJV)

> Fight the good fight of faith, lay hold on eternal life. (1 Timothy 6:12 KJV)

> The blind men came to Him. And Jesus said to them, "Do you believe that I am able to do this?" They said to Him, "Yes, Lord." Then He touched their eyes, saying,

"According to your faith let it be to you." (Matthew 9:28 KJV). And their eyes were opened.

Then Jesus answered and said to her, "O woman, great is your faith! Let it be to you as you desire." (Matthew 15:28 KJV). And her daughter was healed from that very hour.

For she said to herself, "If only I may touch His garment, I shall be made well." But Jesus turned around, and when He saw her He said, "Be of good cheer, daughter; your faith has made you well." (Matthew 9:21 KJV)

Then Jesus said to the centurion, "Go your way; and as you have believed, so let it be done for you." (Matthew 8:13 KJV). And his servant was healed that same hour.

And Jesus answered and said to him, "What do you want Me to do for you?" The blind man said to Him, "Rabboni, that I may receive my sight." Then Jesus said to him, "Go your way; your faith has made you well." (Mark 10:51 KJV). And immediately he received his sight.

Chapter 9

WHY DO SOME PEOPLE RECEIVE HEALING BUT OTHERS DO NOT?

A merry heart makes a cheerful countenance, but by sorrow of the heart the spirit is broken. (Proverbs 15:13 KJV)

Anxiety in the heart of a man causes depression, but a good word makes it glad. (Proverbs 12:25 KJV)

There is one who speaks like the piercings of a sword, but the tongue of the wise promotes health. (Proverbs 12:18)

Notice the first verse says that "envy is rottenness to the bones." This is why the Bible tells us that we are transformed by the "renewing of our minds." God wants to develop and put right thinking into our minds. Having a good, positive mind-set in the Lord may be one of the secrets in being able to have good physical health while we are living on this earth.

The Sin of Gluttony

I know this next topic will be a very sensitive one for many people in this day and age. Many in our society are grossly overweight. For many of these people, certain malfunctions within their bodies cause abnormal weight gain. However, for many others, this weight gain is the result of simply gluttony—overeating and eating the wrong kinds of foods.

With all of the good nutritional information that is now available, we all know what these bad foods are. Also, a ton of educational material is available, showing us what the good foods are and how to structure our diets accordingly to take off a lot of this excess weight.

However, for whatever their personal reasons may be, many people who are overweight simply do not care that they are overeating or that they are grossly overweight. God may have been striving with them, trying to get them to better control their eating habits. However, the human body can only take so much abuse, especially in the area of what we feed it, and sooner or later the breakdown comes. Cancer could set in or a major heart attack could occur. Many different kinds of sicknesses and illnesses can strike our bodies if we do not properly feed and take proper care of them. The Bible tells us that our bodies are the temples of the Holy Spirit.. As such, I believe God the Father wants us to take proper care of them. If we do not and we steadfastly refuse to heed His warnings and promptings, then God may choose not to heal us if we come down with a major sickness as a result of deliberately overeating and abusing our bodies over all those years. The same thing can occur for those who smoke or drink beyond any reasonable moderation. In our walk with the Lord, we have to do the best we can with what we are supposed to be doing for Him.

With none of us being perfect, I believe there is a certain amount of slack with God the Father for some of our weaknesses and character flaws. However, we will get in major trouble with the Lord when we start to push too far with Him and tread past those lines where we should not be going. I believe there is some slack in how we take care of our bodies. I am sure

God is all right with a certain amount of excess body weight due to our own natural imperfections. However, we will get into trouble when we start to go past our own individual slack lines with Him.

If that should happen, then God will start giving us major warning signs and signals that we are getting too far off base. If, after a certain amount of time, we do not heed those warnings and we keep going in the same direction, then God could pull back His hand of protection on us and we could then come down with a major sickness or disease. Remember, some of the above verses state that, if we do what is right in the sight of the Lord, *then* He will not put any of these diseases on us. Going against the Lord by overeating and abusing our bodies is not doing what is right in the Lord, and He thus could pull back His hand of protection on us and our lives. I will leave you with one very interesting verse that tells us to eat only what we really need so that we do not vomit. In other words, we can get physically sick by overeating: "Have you found honey? Eat only as much as you need, lest you be filled with it and vomit" (Proverbs 25:16).

God Is Still Sovereign in All of His Ways

I think that, if you closely study all of the above verses from scripture, the evidence is absolutely overwhelming that God the Father really does want to heal us when we properly approach Him in our prayers. However, another big debate is going on in the body of Christ right now on the subject of divine healing. Many are teaching that it is the will of God that we be healed every single time that we pray and ask for it and that, if we are not healed, then there is something wrong with us. Either our faith was not operating at a high enough level or we may be living in some kind of sin.

Granted, there are times when God may want our faith operating at a higher level. If that is the case, then He may want us to get more into the word to study all of the verses pertaining to divine healing before He will move in to heal us. We also could have some type of sin as discussed above that needs to be taken care of before He will move in to heal us. But what about the Christian who is already operating at a very high level of faith and has a fairly clean slate with the Lord, with no sins that really need to be confessed and forgiven? How do you explain it when they are doing everything right in the Lord and then, all of a sudden, they need a physical healing for themselves but God does not heal them? How do you explain this kind of scenario with the way all of the above verses are worded?

This is just my own humble personal opinion on the matter, but I believe that God is still sovereign in all of His ways, which include when He will manifest the gift of healing on someone. The Bible says that we can know only in part while living down here on this earth. Sometimes God will tell us why He does what He does, and other times He will not.

If God makes a personal decision not to heal people when they are properly approaching Him in prayer for their healing, then I believe there is always a specific reason as to why He chooses not to heal them at that time. Sometimes He will tell us what that reason is, and other times He will not. If He chooses not to tell us, then we have to have full faith and belief that He must have a very good reason for not wanting to give that healing for and then let it go at that. There could be a multitude of reasons why God may choose not to heal someone. I have given this example in several of my other writings, and it is definitely worth repeating for this one.

A woman had been praying for her son's healing. He was only ten years old and had come down with an incurable disease; he was given only a short amount of time to live. God kept telling her that He did not want to heal her son and that she was to let the matter go. The woman would not take no for an answer and kept pressing into God that He would heal her son. Due to her continued persistence, God finally healed the woman's son. However, her testimony ended with her stating that she lived just long enough to watch her son get hanged as a criminal for a murder he committed when he was forty-one years old. God obviously knew what his future had in store for him. He knew that he was going to end up committing this murder. God was actually showing incredible love and mercy by wanting to take him home early with the incurable disease instead of letting him live long enough to commit murder. His mother obviously could not see into his future or understand the big picture, and she thus should have never questioned God's knowledge and wisdom on this matter in the first place since God knew exactly what was going to happen in this boy's future, while she did not.

Bottom line: *God always knows best!* Let His perfect will be done in all matters, which will include whom He will decide to heal and whom He will not decide to heal.

I know many people have had their minds really messed up when, for whatever reason, God has chosen not to heal them, and then another Christian comes along and starts trying to place a guilt trip on them, telling them that either their faith was not operating at a high enough level or that there must be something in their personal lives that was preventing God from wanting to heal them.

As stated earlier, sometimes this may be true, but other times it may not be true. If there are no blocks or hindrances in that person's life, then God is choosing not to heal for another reason. If you are not getting a healing for yourself or someone else you're praying for, then I would press into God and ask Him why He is not moving in to heal. Ask Him to show you if there are any blocks or hindrances that have to be dealt with. If He tells you that there are none but that He has chosen not to heal at this time, then trust that He has a very good reason for not wanting to move in with His healing power and let it go at that. It could be that person's time to go home to be with Him, even if that person is still young, like in the story above. I will end this section with a very good verse from scripture that tells us that God will have mercy on whom He chooses to have mercy. I believe this is one of the verses from scripture that really emphasizes the sovereignty of God and that no one is going to tell Him how to run His universe.

> For He says to Moses, "I will have mercy on whomever I
> will have mercy, and I will have compassion on whomever
> I will have compassion.... Therefore He has mercy on
> whom He wills.... But indeed, O' man, who are you to
> reply against God? Will the thing formed say to him who
> formed it, "Why have you made me like this?" Doesn't
> the potter have power over the clay" (Romans 9:15–21)

Though there are times when God will decide not to heal for whatever His personal reasons may be, at other times He will move in to heal if you properly approached Him in your prayers. Since God is totally sovereign in His very nature and in all of His ways, this means you never know when He may move in to heal someone. This is why you should never be afraid to approach God's throne boldly and with confidence if either you or someone you know needs a physical healing from Him. You have absolutely nothing to lose in trying and everything to gain by pressing in. For those of you who would really like to get serious with the Lord on being able to get more healings to manifest from Him for either yourself or any of your loved ones, it would be my strong recommendation that you type or handwrite out all of the scripture verses listed in this chapter and put them on index cards. If you are willing to do this, then you will have right at your fingertips all of the major healing verses of the Bible to use in your own personal healing prayers to God the Father.

Simply pick the verses that will apply to the specific situation that you are dealing with, and then storm the gates of heaven asking God to move in to heal based upon the wording of many of these verses. God loves it when you quote His own Word back to Him. This shows Him that you have been doing your homework and that you are seeking to learn more about Him and this subject by studying and meditating on these kinds of verses. This kind of intense, seeking activity may be just enough to get God the Father to want to heal you or the person you may be praying for!

Read these scriptures until you memorize them. Meditate on them as you pray at least three times a day, and then watch God.

> Surely he hath borne our griefs, and carried our sorrows: yet we did esteem him stricken, smitten of God, and afflicted. But he was wounded for our transgressions, he was bruised for our iniquities: the chastisement of our peace was upon him; and with his stripes we are healed. (Isaiah 53:4–5 KJV)

> When the evening was come, they brought unto him many that were possessed with devils: and he cast out the spirits with his word, and healed all that were sick. That it might be fulfilled which was spoken by Esaias the prophet, saying, Himself took our infirmities, and bare our sicknesses. (Matthew 8:16–17 KJV)

Chapter 10

WHAT TO DO WHEN YOUR SYMPTOMS RETURN

Bless the LORD, O my soul, and forget not all his benefits. Who forgiveth all thine iniquities; who healeth all thy diseases. (Psalm 103:2 KJV)

Who his own self bare our sins in his own body on the tree, that we, being dead to sins, should live unto righteousness: by whose stripes ye were healed. (Peter 2:24 KJV)

Christ hath redeemed us from the curse of the law, being made a curse for us: for it is written, Cursed is every one that hangeth on a tree. (Galatians 3:13 KJV)

And said, If thou wilt diligently hearken to the voice of the LORD thy God, and wilt do that which is right in his sight, and wilt give ear to his commandments, and keep all his statutes, I will put none of these diseases upon thee, which I have brought upon the Egyptians: for I am the LORD that healeth thee. (Exodus 15:26 KJV)

He sent out his word and healed them; he rescued them from the grave. (Psalm 107:20 NIV)

And ye shall serve the LORD your God, and he shall bless thy bread, and thy water; and I will take sickness away from the midst of thee. There shall nothing cast their young, nor be barren, in thy land: the number of thy days I will fulfill. (Exodus 23:25–26 KJV)

So is my word that goes out from my mouth: It will not return to me empty, but will accomplish what I desire and achieve the purpose for which I sent it. (Isaiah 55:11 NIV)

For the eyes of the LORD run to and fro throughout the whole earth, to shew himself strong on the behalf of those whose heart is perfect toward him. Herein thou hast done foolishly: therefore from henceforth thou shalt have wars. (Chronicles 16:9 KJV)

There shall no evil befall thee, neither shall any plague come nigh thy dwelling. With long life will I satisfy him, and shew him my salvation. (Psalm 91:10–16)

If you, then, though you are evil, know how to give good gifts to your children, how much more will your Father in heaven give good gifts to those who ask him! (Matthew 7:11 NIV)

Every good and perfect gift is from above, coming down from the Father of the heavenly lights, who does not change like shifting shadows. (James 1:17 NIV)

And the LORD will take away from thee all sickness, and will put none of the evil diseases of Egypt, which thou knowest, upon thee. (Deuteronomy 7:15 NIV)

A man with leprosy came and knelt before him and said, "Lord, if you are willing, you can make me clean." Jesus reached out his hand and touched the man. "I am willing," he said. "Be clean!" Immediately he was cleansed of his leprosy. (Matthew 8:2–3 NIV)

But to you who fear My name The Sun of Righteousness shall arise With healing in His wings; And you shall go out And grow fat like stall-fed calves. (Malachi 4:2 NKJV)

How God anointed Jesus of Nazareth with the Holy Spirit and power, and how he went around doing good and healing all who were under the power of the devil, because God was with him. (Acts 10:38 NIV)

The thief comes only to steal and kill and destroy; I have come that they may have life, and have it to the full. (John 10:10 NIV)

Come, and let us return to the LORD; For He has torn, but He will heal us; He has stricken, but He will bind us up. (Hosea 6:1 NKJV)

My son, give attention to my words; Incline your ear to my sayings. Do not let them depart from your eyes; Keep them in the midst of your heart; For they are life to those who find them, And health to all their flesh. Save me, and I shall be saved, For You are my praise. (Proverbs 4:20–22 NKJV)

"For I will restore health to you And heal you of your wounds," says the LORD, "Because they called you an outcast saying: 'This is Zion; No one seeks her.'" (Jeremiah 30:17 NKJV)

He that spared not his own Son, but delivered him up for us all, how shall he not with him also freely give us all things? (Romans 8:32 KJV)

There shall not be male or female barren among you. (Deuteronomy 7:14 KJV)

With his stripes we are healed. (Isaiah 53:5 KJV)

I will never forget thy precepts: for with them thou hast quickened me. (Psalm 119:93 KJV)

If the Son therefore shall make you free, ye shall be free indeed. (John 8:36 KJV)

For the law of the Spirit of life in Christ Jesus hath made me free from the law of sin and death. (Romans 8:2 KJV)

Now thanks be unto God, which always causeth us to triumph in Christ. (2 Corinthians 2:14 KJV)

For this purpose the Son of God was manifested, that he might destroy the works of the devil. (1 John 3:8 KJV)

Confess your faults one to another, and pray one for another, that ye may be healed. The effectual fervent prayer of a righteous man availeth much. (James 5:16 KJV)

He giveth power to the faint; and to them that have no might he increaseth strength. (Isaiah 40:29 KJV)

I will restore health unto thee, and I will heal thee of thy wounds. (Jeremiah 30:17 KJV)

The Spirit also helpeth our infirmities. (Romans 8:26 KJV)

They that wait upon the LORD shall renew their strength. (Isaiah 40:31 KJV)

Every plant, which my heavenly Father hath not planted, shall be rooted up. (Matthew 15:13 KJV)

He that raised up Christ from the dead shall also quicken your mortal bodies by his Spirit that dwelleth in you. (Romans 8:11 KJV)

Be not wise in thine own eyes: fear the LORD, and depart from evil. It shall be health to thy navel, and marrow to thy bones. (Proverbs 3:7–8 KJV)

My son, attend to my words; incline thine ear unto my sayings. Let them not depart from thine eyes; keep them in the midst of thine heart. For they are life unto those that find them, and health to all their flesh. (Proverbs 4:20–22 KJV)

Surely he shall deliver thee from the snare of the fowler, and from the noisome pestilence. (Psalm 91:3 KJV)

Hope thou in God: for I shall yet praise him, who is the health of my countenance, and my God. (Psalm 42:11 KJV)

For God hath not given us the spirit of fear; but of power, and of love, and of a sound mind. (2 Timothy 1:7 KJV)

Behold, I will bring it health and cure, and I will cure them, and will reveal unto them the abundance of peace and truth. (Jeremiah 33:6 KJV)

But the Lord is faithful, who shall establish you, and keep you from evil. (2 Thessalonians 3:3 KJV)

God is our refuge and strength, a very present help in trouble. (Psalm 46:1 KJV)

Cast thy burden upon the LORD, and he shall sustain thee: he shall never suffer the righteous to be moved. (Psalm 55:22 KJV)

O keep my soul, and deliver me: let me not be ashamed; for I put my trust in thee. (Psalm 25:20 KJV)

For the Lord GOD will help me; therefore shall I not be confused: therefore have I set my face like a flint, and I know that I shall not be ashamed. (Isaiah 50:7 KJV)

Heal me, O LORD, and I shall be healed; save me, and I shall be saved: for thou art my praise. (Jeremiah 17:14 KJV)

I am afflicted very much: quicken me, O LORD, according unto thy word. (Psalm 119:107 KJV)

My help cometh from the LORD, which made heaven and earth. (Psalm 121:2 KJV)

This is my comfort in my affliction: for thy word hath quickened me. (Psalm 119:50 KJV)

Peace, peace to him that is far off, and to him that is near, saith the LORD; and I will heal him. (Isaiah 57:19 KJV)

I believed, therefore have I spoken: I was greatly afflicted. (Psalm 116:10 KJV)

When thou passest through the waters, I will be with thee; and through the rivers, they shall not overflow thee. (Isaiah 43:2 KJV)

I will put none of these diseases upon thee ... for I am the LORD that healeth thee. (Exodus 15:26 KJV)

Chapter 11

AUTHOR'S STORY

E phesians 1:17–19 says, "The God of our Lord Jesus Christ, the father of glory, may give to you the spirit of wisdom and revelation in the knowledge of him. The eyes of your understanding being enlightened that you may know what is the hope of his calling, what are the riches of the glory of his inheritance in the saints, and what is the exceeding greatness of his power toward us who believe, according to the working of his mighty power" (KJV).

The book of Mark does not say that those who believe will lay hands on the sick and, on occasion, they may recover. No, it states that they will lay hands on the sick, and they will recover (Mark 16:18 NKJV). Most Christians believe that God can heal, no matter what the denomination they belong to or what church they attend. So why aren't people being healed within the church around the world? Why aren't Christians laying hands on the sick and seeing them recover? The scripture says these signs will follow those who believe (Mark 16:17 NKJV).

In 1997, I was diagnosed with diabetes, and I was completely healed from this during a church service while I was singing on the praise team. And in 2011 I began to suffer with my left knee. It began swelling and continued to swell. So I decided to make an appointment with my doctor, who in turn sent me to a knee specialist, who told me that my knee was completely blown out and that I needed to stop working in construction. The doctor gave me some medication to reduce the swelling, but the medicine kept raising my blood pressure.

So I needed to find a new career after receiving this devastating news. All I could do was quit my job because I could no longer walk on this leg. I remember going home that evening, getting on my knees, and crying continuously, thinking, *What am I going to do now?* I felt that I was too old to start a new career this late in life. And I was not about to get a knee replacement. I had seen too many people who had those knee surgeries come out worse. I remember going around preaching while hopping on one leg.

Then, depression started to set in as the bills began piling up, and then my house went into foreclosure. I remember saying, "Why me, Lord?" That's when I thought, *I just finished writing a book about healing. Now I really have to put in practice the things that I just wrote about.* It did not take me long to remember that King David stated that sometimes you have to encourage yourself in the Lord, so I began to meditate upon the goodness of the Lord Jesus Christ, how good He has been to me, and how He has always opened doors for me. Then one day I received a call from a construction company with an offer to go to a job out of town to make a whole lot of money. I accepted it, but everyone thought that I was crazy for taking this job with a blown-out knee. Nevertheless, I began to exercise my faith in God, and as I drove out of town to the job site on the first night I started work, God healed me completely. Thank God! I believe that God acted on my faith in Him, which I showed by taking the job against all odds and not listening to what others were telling me. Years later, I am still working on the same knee that the doctor said would never be the same again. Just always remember that it is not over until God says it's over. When all else fails, God steps in.

Chapter 12

PACEMAKER REMOVED

---

n 1988, I was twenty-six years old and considered myself to be in pretty good health. I worked out regularly and tried to eat as healthfully as possible. I had no health problems, and I was not on any kind of medication. I was working for an aerospace company in San Pedro, California, as an inventory specialist. My job was not stressful in any way. I was married with three children, going to work every day and living for God.

Then one day, out of the blue, my dad was diagnosed with a heart condition and was placed in the hospital. Doctors began running all sorts of tests to see why he was having dizzy spells and light-headedness, and it was not long before the cardiologists were able to diagnose my dad's heart condition.

He was diagnosed with tachycardia-bradycardia syndrome, a condition in which the heart sometimes beats too fast and sometimes beats too slow. So the doctors decided to place a pacemaker to control his heartbeat. After my dad had the operation, I clearly remember going to the hospital to pray for him. Little did I know that, three months later, I would be in the hospital having the same procedure done myself.

My dad once told me a story about three of his cousins. One was seventeen years old, one was nineteen, and the other one was around twenty-one or twenty-four years old. All three of them died suddenly in their sleep. It was never determined what may have caused their deaths. It happened in the forties and fifties, when they did not have as many ways of diagnosing these kinds of problems as we do now.

For me, it all began on a Saturday night after I ate several slices of my favorite pizza. I went to sleep. Later, I suddenly woke up, went to the bathroom, and immediately started feeling very dizzy and light-headed. It felt like I was about to pass out, so I picked up the phone and dialed 9-1-1. The paramedics and firefighters quickly responded. They came in, checked all of my vitals, and stated that all of my vitals were good but, as a precaution, they would take me to the nearest hospital in Long Beach, California.

Once there, doctors started running tests and examining me. They checked all of my arteries to see if there were any blockages. All of that came back negative, so around the fourth day of my hospitalization and having all sorts of tests performed on my heart, the cardiologists decided to release me. I started getting ready to go home but began feeling really sleepy, so I decided to lay down to wait for the doctor to sign my final release from the hospital.

All of the sudden, doctors and nurses from all over the hospital had converged on my room. It was a code blue. When I woke up, I saw doctors and nurses standing over me. One asked, "How do you feel?"

I said I felt great and asked, "What is the problem?"

The doctor stated, "Your heart stopped completely while you were asleep." They gave me a shot to keep my heart pumping really fast to keep it from slowing down and stopping again.

The next day a cardiology specialist came to my room and said, "It was a good thing that we did not send you home yesterday with this problem because, with these kinds of problems, people usually don't wake up. They simply die in their sleep." Then my mind went back to the story that my dad had told me about the three cousins who had mysteriously died in their sleep. I told the cardiologist about them and added that, three months earlier, my dad had the same problem and had a pacemaker installed. So after my heart stopped the third time, the cardiologists ran numerous tests and decided that I needed to have a pacemaker installed in my heart as well. I agreed to have the procedure done. While I was in the operating room, I woke up right in the middle of the surgery. I will never forget the look on the anesthesiologist's and all of those doctors' and nurses' faces. I asked them, "What are y'all doing to me?" and the doctor asked me, "Do you feel anything?"

I replied, "Yes, it feels as though you are sewing on me." That's when I saw the cardiologist look over at the anesthesiologist and gave him a thumbs-down signal. I guess that meant to give me some more medicine to knock me out completely. The next time I woke up, they took me to the ICU so that I could be monitored around the clock. I remember one particular nurse coming to my room and saying, "You were not supposed to wake up in the middle of surgery. Someone completely dropped the ball, and more than likely it was the anesthesiologist."

After three days, I was released to go home from the hospital. I went back to work and started living a normal life once again. I had no limitations except for going near microwave ovens and certain X-ray machines. I went every six months to have the pacemaker checked to make sure it was doing what it was designed to do, but after a while I completely stopped going to the doctor. Ten years later, I decided to go and have the pacemaker checked, and the doctors found that it had stopped working. The battery was completely dead. I had no idea that the battery only lasted for several years and had to be changed. I remember the cardiologists being so angry and upset with me. They told me, "You have to be more responsible." They said that I needed to keep track of and follow up on all of my appointments from then on, so I agreed.

The doctor then told me that the pacemaker had been dead for several years, so I asked why I needed it if, all of this time, it had not even been working. They told me that it was better to have it and not need it than to need it and not have it, which made lots of sense to me at that time. By then my faith in God had really grown, and I started to tell them to just remove it entirely. But I listened to others who did not have any faith in God as they talked me out of it.

So every five years, I would go in to have a battery replacement. I would stay in the hospital for only one to two days and then be released as long as I didn't have any complications from the procedure. But one interesting thing about the pacemaker is that, when I would go to have it checked, it would give dates and times of everything that went on within my heart, like when my heart would slow or speeds up. It was designed to turn on if my heart rate dropped below sixty-five beats per minute.

Well, in 2017, around thirty years after I had it installed, I began to notice that my skin over where the pacemaker had been placed started itching a lot. Then I noticed a little spot that later became a small hole. At the time, I was working in El Dorado, Arkansas, as a pipe fitter, so I went to CVS drugstore, bought a few bandages and some wraps, and covered it up until I could get to my cardiologist.

I began to notice that, each day, the hole got bigger and bigger until, one day, while changing the bandages, I was able to see the wiring on the pacemaker itself. And believe it or not, I really wasn't alarmed about this. So after the job ended, I loaded up my toolbox and headed back home to Louisiana, where I decided to go to the emergency room.

The nurse in the emergency room took one look at my chest and immediately checked me in to see the doctor right away. Cardiologists from all over the hospital came to the emergency room to see me. They then sent me to their main hospital by emergency ambulance to try and find out why the pacemaker had completely come out and was hanging by the wires that went into my heart. After running several tests, the cardiologists and infectious disease doctor said that I had one of the worst bacterial infections that they had ever seen and that the entire pacemaker was infected and had to be immediately removed.

I was diagnosed with a very serious staph infection by the name of Orris-B. Whenever you have a staph infection that bad, sometimes your body tries to reject foreign objects. This staph infection was causing my body to completely reject the pacemaker, which is truly amazing to me. It would be one week before they could get a special cardiologist to go in and remove the entire pacemaker. They were easy to put in but very hard to remove, especially after having it in for thirty long years. I found out that only a small number of cardiologists were capable of performing this type of surgery because it was considered to be extremely dangerous. So after the doctors finished running all of the tests on my heart, they all decided that I did not need the pacemaker anymore and that they would not put a new one inside of me.

The day of the surgery, I had been fasting and praying for a complete miracle from God. I was praying that, when the doctors went in to remove the pacemaker, they would find that it had already been removed by God. However, that did not happen. The infectious disease doctor could not understand why I was not running any fever from all of the staph infection that was in my body. The entire surgery took about ten hours to perform. Once it was completed, I was placed in ICU, and after three days the doctors decided to send me home with forty-five days of intravenous antibiotics. After that, I was able to go back to work. It's been seven years now since I had the pacemaker removed, and I haven't had any more complications.

I truly give Jesus Christ all of the glory and honor for healing my body completely and making me whole once again because I believe with all of my heart that God is a healer. Doctors stated they had never had a case like mine. This is why so many doctors and cardiologists from all over the country kept pouring into my room to see me, take pictures, and ask me questions concerning my case. The doctors said that this was a new one for the textbooks.

One more thing I forgot to add: after the surgery to have the pacemaker removed, doctors were astounded that I had no pain—none whatsoever. I did not have to take any pain medicine. They could not understand, especially after all of the cutting that they had performed on my chest area. And not once did I ever run a fever. Thank God for that. Here are the pictures that were taken by the doctors. I must warn you: the pictures are very hard to look at and very graphic.

Grant Bruce Scan on 2/22/2016
by Julia B. Garcia-Diaz, MD

Grant, Bruce Scan on 2/1/2016 by Sarah M. Lillis, MD of Under pacemaker

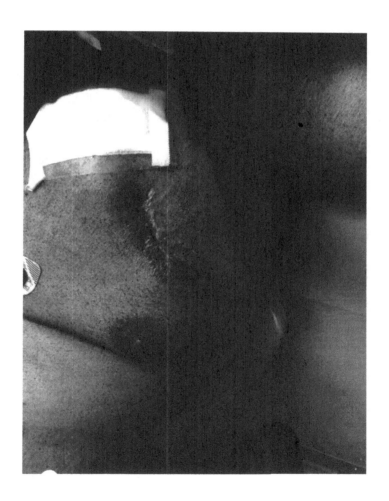

Grant, Bruce Scan on 2/22/2016
by Julia B. Garcia-Diaz, MD

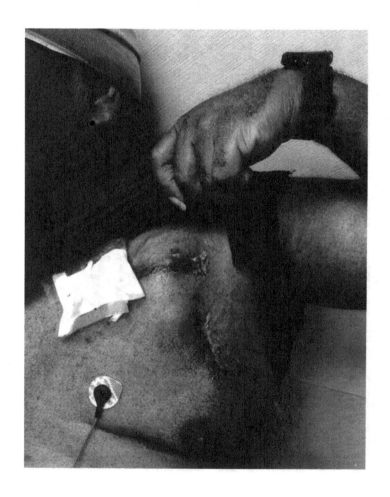

Grant Bruce Scan on 2/10/2016 by Janet L. White, APRN, ANP

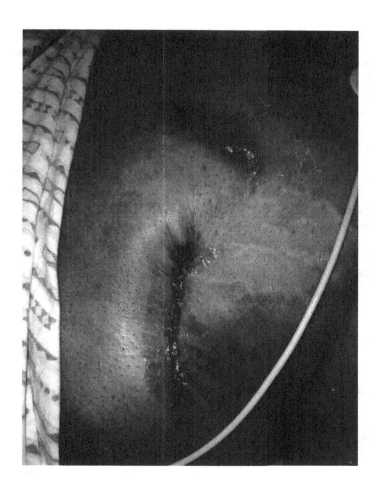

Grant, Bruce Scan on 2/1/2016 by Sarah M. Lillis, MD of Pacemaker

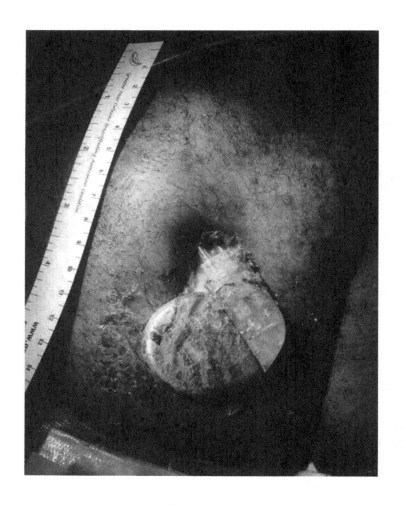

Grant, Bruce Scan on 2/1/2016 by Sarah M. Lillis, MD of Pacemaker

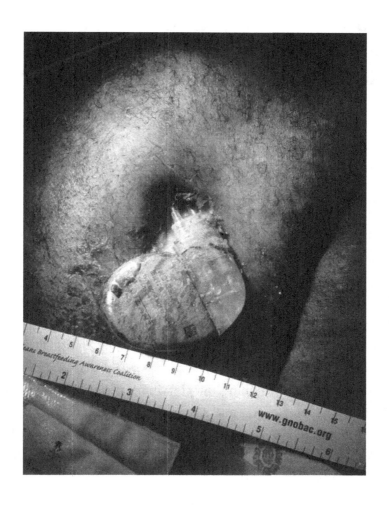

Chapter 13

ARE YOU WILLING TO GET RID OF EVERYTHING THAT YOU KNOW IS MAKING YOU SICK?

I n 3 John 2 (KJV), we read, "I wish above all things that thou mayest prosper and be in health, even as thy soul prospers. So as you can see it is in God's perfect will for all of us." To be prosperous and to have perfect health—it was in God's original plan. Now, once you get sick, there is always the power of healing and supernatural miracles, even though some today might not think so.

However, the Bible states in Hebrews 13:8 (KJV), "Jesus Christ is the same yesterday, today and forever." To me this means that God's word has not changed since the beginning and He will not change his Word. God's word will always remain the same. If this is the case and if God's desire in the beginning was for us to have good health and walk in success, then it is God's will and desire for us as believers to have the same blessings today.

First, let's look at what the dictionary says on exactly what a miracle means. It says that a miracle is a surprising and welcome event that is not explicable by natural or scientific means and is therefore considered to be the work of a divine agency, so the question is, Does God still perform miracles today? And the answer to that question is absolutely yes. The reason I can say this without a shadow of doubt is because, when you look at me, you are looking at a miracle.

My opinion is that you must be willing to get rid of all of the things you know of that might be causing you to be sick most of the time. When people are diagnosed with life-threatening illnesses, the first question we ask is, "Why me?" Well, the reason most people even get sick in the first place is because, if we are totally honest, we don't take care of our bodies as we should. Our bodies were designed with extraordinary healing capabilities, but because of all of the foods that we continually put in our bodies and the lack of proper rest and nutrition, we often find ourselves not feeling well or at our best—always tired, lacking energy, and not to mention substance abuse such as excessive alcohol intake, tobacco use, and excessive overeating. God clearly states in the book of Leviticus what we should and should not eat. However, most people will say that it is in the Old Testament and that it's OK to eat whatever you want to eat as long as you pray over it first. This is why so many people are in such poor health.

God created us, and I believe that God knows more about our bodies than we will ever know. I believe that this is why God instructed the children of Israel on what to eat and what not to eat. It should be common sense not to put some things into our bodies, but we just keep on doing it anyway. We each have only one body, and when it's gone, that's it. There are no spare bodies, so at all costs, we need to learn how to take care of our bodies with good nutrition and exercise along with maintaining the proper weight and size. We cannot continue to abuse our bodies and expect good results. It is just like a car—if you don't do regular maintenance on your vehicle, it will continue to break down at unexpected times. But if you take care of your car, it will most likely take care of you.

It is the same with our bodies. We cannot expect to eat hamburgers and french fries and drink soft drinks every day and expect to have energy and strength. Isn't it amazing how most of the foods that we eat that taste good to us are usually the same foods that are bad for us? And the foods that taste bad to us are usually the foods that are the healthiest for us. Think about it—who wouldn't want a big ol' juicy hamburger with lots of cheese on it? The experts say that some foods that we eat are directly related to certain cancers. We know this and are yet still willing to take chances on what we eat. Even after we have spent years abusing and neglecting our bodies and begin to develop all sorts of health issues, God can choose to heal us. In most cases, wouldn't you rather start taking care of your body so that you don't have to one day pray to God for your healing miracle? Why should God want to heal you from lung cancer if you knowingly and willingly smoke up to five packs of cigarettes per day? Or why should He heal your cirrhosis if you spent years abusing alcohol and destroying your liver? Let's just say that God chooses to heal you from lung cancer. Will you be willing to get rid of the thing that gave you cancer in the first place? Would you stop the excessive alcohol abuse or the extreme overeating if he healed you? For instance, if you are extremely overweight and are constantly eating the wrong foods and, as a result, develop diabetes, high blood pressure, and other issues, can God heal you? Absolutely yes. But are you willing to make the necessary adjustments by starting to eat the right foods, exercise, and lose weight? This is a question that we should all be asking ourselves.

Most people don't start eating right, exercising, and taking care of their bodies until they are diagnosed with some kind of disease, and I must say that I am extremely guilty. If I can be totally honest with myself, it's time to stop making excuses. It's time for all of us to start taking good care of our bodies. One thing about it is that it is never too late to start taking care of our only bodies, so together we can do this. Let's pray to God to give us the help and the strength that we need in order to accomplish this very important goal. We must do it not only for ourselves but for all of those who love us. I don't know about you, but I want to be around to see all of my grandchildren and great-grandchildren grow up. Our bodies are the temple of the Holy Spirit, and we must start treating it well.

God normally does for us the things that we cannot do for ourselves, but for some things that we ask God to do for us, He expects us to do ourselves, like taking care of the bodies that He blessed us with. We have to make up our minds, start doing the things that we know are good for our bodies, and stop doing those things that we know are unhealthy and detrimental to our health. Once we start taking care of our bodies, I truly believe with all of my heart that God will do the rest.

Father, in the name of Jesus, please help us this day to make the right choices when it comes to our health. I pray that all of those who are reading this book and struggling with any and all unwanted addictions, please, Lord Jesus, give them the courage and the strength to make the necessary change over their lives and to lay aside every weight and every sin that so easily entangles them. Help us to run with patience the race that is set before us (Hebrews 12:1). In Jesus's mighty name, amen.

Chapter 14

CORRECTING AN ABUSE
OF THE LORD'S SUPPER

In 1 Corinthians 11:17–34 (KJV), we read,

I have no praise for you for your meetings do more harm than good. In the first place. I hear that when you come together as a church. There are divisions among you, and to some extent. I believe it. No doubt there have to be differences among you to show which of you have God's approval. So then when you come together. It is not the Lord's supper, you eat. For when you are eating, some of you go ahead with your own private suppers. As a result, one person remains hungry and another gets drunk. Don't you have homes to eat and drink in? Or do you despise the church of God by merely humiliating those who have nothing? What shall I say to you? Shall I praise you? Certainly not in this matter! For I received from the Lord. What I also passed on to you; the Lord Jesus on the night he was betrayed, took bread, and when he had given thanks, he broke it and said, this is my body, which is for you; do this in remembrance of me. In the same way, after supper he took the cup, saying, this cup is the new covenant in my blood; do this, whenever you drink it, in remembrance of me'. For whenever you eat this bread and drink this cup, you proclaim the Lord's death until he comes. So then, whoever eats the bread or drinks the cup of the Lord in an unworthy manner will be guilty of sinning against the body and blood of the Lord. Everyone ought to examine themselves before they eat the bread and drink from the cup. For those who eat and drink without discerning the body of Christ eat and drink judgment on themselves. That is why many among you are weak and sick, and a number of you have fallen asleep (Died). But if we were more discerning with regard to ourselves, we would not come under such judgment. Nevertheless, when we are judged in this way by the Lord, we are being disciplined, so that we will not be finally condemned with the world. So then, my brothers and sisters, when you gather, you should all eat together. Anyone who is hungry should eat something at home, so that when you meet together. It may not result in judgment. And when I come. I will give father directors.

Back when I first invited Jesus Christ into my heart as my personal savior, we in the church of God in Christ really took communion time very seriously, as it is serious. I was told that this was a covenant that we were to take very, very seriously, and it was not to be played with. If we knew that we were not right and had sin in our lives, then we were instructed by our elders in the church not to—I repeat, *not to*—take communion. However, nowadays people just don't take communion very seriously. Most people nowadays live any kind of old raggedy lives. They live like the devil throughout the week, living in adultery and fornicating, and then go to church on Sunday and take communion without having any plan to change and get their hearts right with God. They do not understand the seriousness of knowingly taking communion and living in a life of sin. The reason most people do it is a lack of seriousness being taught among our leaders. Most leaders treat communion as though it's just another routine act, but I am here to tell you that it is not and that communion should be handled with utmost urgency and reverence to God. I don't care how you might try to dress it up, but my Bible clearly states that many are weak and sickly among you and that many sleep, which is interpreted as dying. I truly believe that we as leaders have to start stressing the importance of communion and that people cannot knowingly violate God's laws, commandments, and principles by knowingly living in sin and taking communion. We as a church have to start living in a continuous state of repentance and not be so complacent when it comes to the things of God. This might be the reason so many people are sick as well and cannot seem to get their healing. Always make sure that you are in right relationship with the Lord Jesus Christ as our Savior. Amen.

Chapter 15

I SURVIVED COVID-19 THREE TIMES

I t all started around February 2020, when I first started hearing about the coronavirus. I had heard people talk about the virus on the news, but at that time, I really didn't believe it. Some people weren't really taking it seriously. But then I was at work one day and noticed that the company I worked for had brought in a lot of extra employees to clean. These people were cleaning tables, doorknobs, and chairs and mopping floors. Little did I know that someone had been diagnosed with COVID-19 and the company was keeping it a secret because they did not want to alarm the employees.

I noticed one day that the young man with whom I shared a desk had been coughing and sneezing a lot and appeared to be very sick. I joked with him one day, saying, "You need to get away from me because I believe that you have the coronavirus." He laughed and said, "I just have a regular cold." Well, a few days later, I began feeling sick. I was not running any fever, but I did have a pretty bad cough and a loss of appetite. I started having difficulty breathing, and around the third day I went to sleep and woke up gasping for air. I felt as though someone was choking me. I could not get any air, so I got up, put my clothes on, and went to the nearest hospital. I was immediately admitted on March 3, and while I was laying there in the bed struggling to breathe, I began praying to God for relief while the doctors were running all kinds of tests on me. My heart rate was extremely high, and it felt as though someone was sitting on my chest.

While I was lying in bed, I started feeling exhausted. Somehow I managed to fall asleep, and while sleeping I had a vision that Jesus Christ walked into my room and touched me on my head. I heard a voice saying that three people shall go into the hospital but only two are coming out. When I woke up from that vision or dream, I began to think about the two people I knew who were close to me and also in the hospital with the coronavirus, struggling for their lives. One was my mother-in-law, who I love very much, and the other was my wife's first cousin, a young man.

Then I heard the Spirit of God say to me, "You will not have to go through this one," and all of the sudden all my vitals, heart rate, and oxygen level returned to normal. At the same time, the emergency room doctor walked in and stated, "I was sitting there looking at the monitors on you, Mr. Grant, when all of the sudden it appeared that everything went normal." That's when I started thanking God Almighty.

The hospital released me to go home after five hours in the emergency room. So I went home feeling great and went to bed. The next morning, I received a call from the doctor saying that my COVID-19 test came back positive and that I needed to go into quarantine for fourteen days. So I did, and each day for those fourteen days, someone at the hospital called to see how I was doing and if my symptoms had worsened. After those fourteen days of being locked up in a room, I decided to quarantine another fourteen days to be on the safe side.

After quarantining for twenty-eight days, I came out. During that time, my mother-in-law had passed away while in the hospital and my wife's first cousin had been sent home after being on a ventilator for two months; he went on to make a full recovery. Since then, the church that I attend has lost many of our members to the coronavirus.

I don't quite understand how it all works—how some people who got the virus have died while others lived. My mother-in-law, her pastor, and his wife all passed away from this terrible virus. I can truly say that I was worried at first because I am considered overweight and take pills for high blood pressure. But then God came into my room and reassured me that I would be all right. Every day I have thanked Him for allowing me to live, for saving me and sparing my life.

I thank my Lord and Savior Jesus Christ for His grace and mercy toward me and for allowing me to live. He said, "You shall live and not die to declare the works of the Lord."

God Almighty.

ABOUT THE AUTHOR

My name is Bruce A. Grant, and my wife's name is Angela D. Grant. We have been married for thirty-nine years, and we are both ordained elders in the Full Gospel Baptist Church. We have four wonderful children, along with seven grandchildren.

In 1982, I received Jesus Christ into my heart. For two years, I was the leader of a group of street evangelists who would go out into the highways and byways once a week to reach the lost. I witnessed many lives changed through the power of Jesus Christ. We would visit hospitals and convalescent homes. We would visit the projects to preach the gospel of Jesus Christ, feed the hungry, and hand out donations that had been given to us from the local stores.

From 1984 to 1988, I served faithfully as the president of Young People Willing Workers (YPWW) in the Church of God in Christ organization, where my wife also served faithfully as the sunshine band president, working with children aged three to twelve. In 1997, my wife and I became youth pastors for the Full Gospel ministries. For ten years we served faithfully, and from 2007 to present, we serve as leaders over the ministers and elders.

Printed in the United States
by Baker & Taylor Publisher Services

Author Bruce Grant has experienced nearly every sickness imaginable, and the Lord delivered him through each one. He's stood in long prayer lines throughout America praying for a healing. No one likes to be sick, and Grant felt like he was suffering from some ailment all the time. Then, in 1984, he attended a Kenneth Hagin crusade in California. Grant learned how to pray to God for himself, and he started reading the word of God to see what God has to say about healing.

In *Jesus Sent Your Healing—Now Receive It,* Grant uses his personal experiences and a host of Bible scriptures to help you understand what to do when you are sick and need healing from God. He shares how he witnessed God's amazing power through healing manifestations.

Bruce Grant and his wife, Angela D. Grant, are both ordained elders in the full gospel church. Married for thirty-nine years, they have four children and seven grandchildren. In 1982, he received Jesus Christ into his heart and felt the call of God to start a street evangelist team. Grant also served as a youth pastor for ten years.

WESTBOW
PRESS®
A DIVISION OF THOMAS NELSON
& ZONDERVAN

U.S. $13.99

ISBN 979-8-3850-3420-
5 1 3 9

9 798385 034208

POWER UP

7 TRANSFORMATIONAL STEPS
TO OWN YOUR POWER AND HAVE
MORE JOY IN YOUR LIFE!

JACKIE CAWLEY, DO, MBA